YUG PEOPLE

APJ ABDUL KALAM

Designed by: Heta Bhuta
Illustrations: Arushi Gupta

Once upon a time in Rameswaram, a little boy named Avul Pakir Jainulabdeen Abdul Kalam was born on October 15th, 1931. His father was a boat owner named Jainulabdeen who ferried Hindu devotees to and from Rameshwaram Temple, and his mother was a homemaker named Ashiamma.

He had four elder brothers and a sister. Although Abdul lived in a joint family that endured financial difficulties, one day he would transcend his humble beginnings and emerge as India's Missile Man and also the 11th President.

Let's start at the beginning of his incredible journey!

From a young age, Abdul's access to food and electricity remained limited at home. Little Abdul's day would begin early morning at 4 am and end at night right next to a kerosene lamp his mother kept lit especially for him because he was passionate about studying.

Somehow, he took time out to distribute newspapers to raise funds, too.

When Abdul's teacher explained how a bird flies, he dreamed of making something that would fly when he grew up. He studied aerospace engineering and obtained a PhD in physics.

Although he wanted to become a fighter pilot, he missed the opportunity by a slim margin. This loss became our nation's gain - Abdul was meant to transform all of India through science and technology!

PhD PHYSICS
ABDUL KALAM

DRDO
AGNI
BHARAT
AKASH
PRITHVI

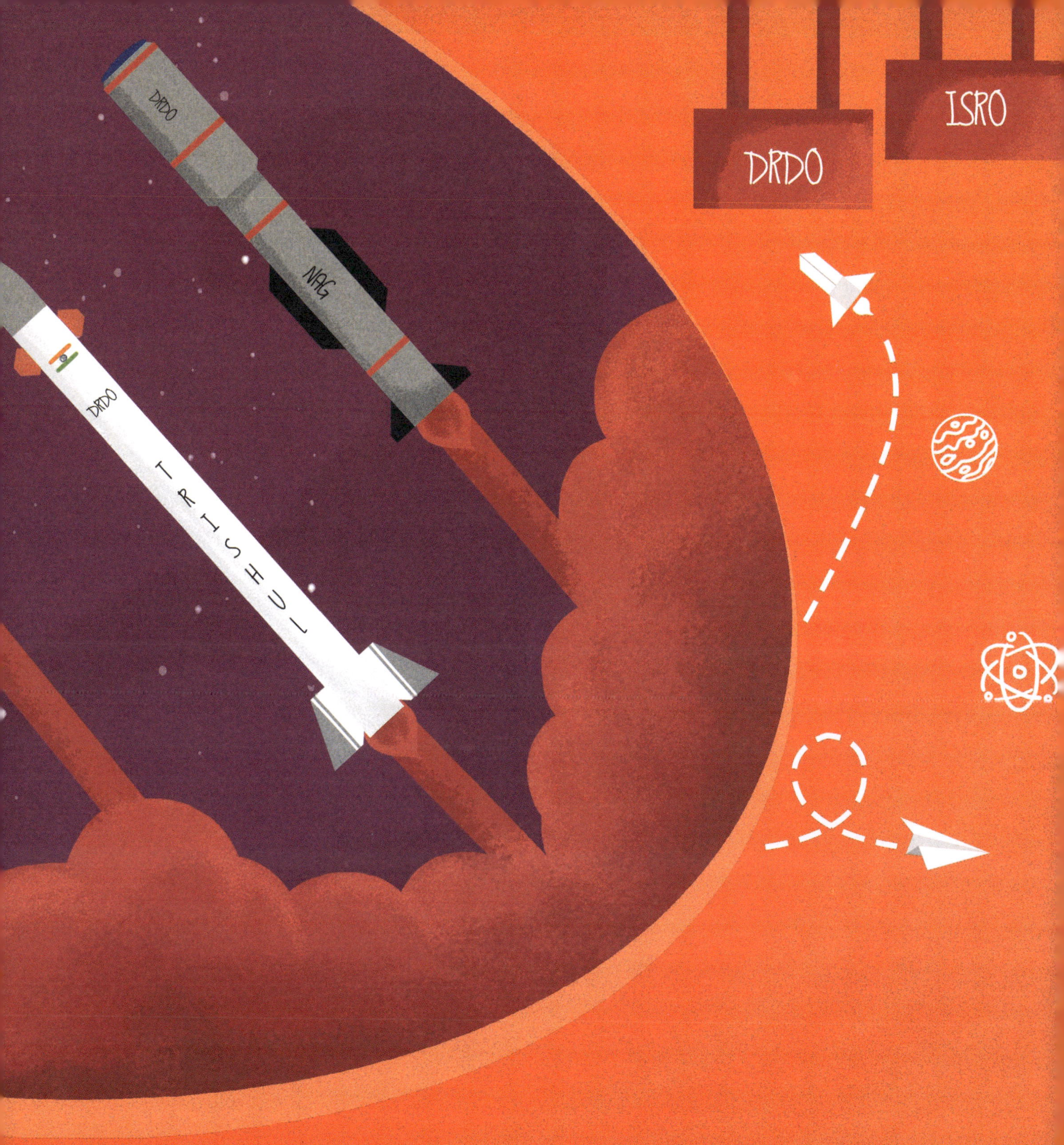

Abdul did amazing work with the Defense Research & Development Organization (DRDO) and Indian Space Research Organization (ISRO) - he developed missiles for India, including the much talked about Prithvi, Agni, Trishul, Akash and Nag!

In 1998, Kalam decided it was high time India announced its nuclear presence to the world. As the chief of DRDO, he personally supervised the Pokhran-II explosions, which marked the true beginning of a new, exciting era for India. Kalam was a national hero! And, yet, he remained compassionate toward everyone around him.

Chief of DRDO

In July 2002, Abdul's brilliant mind and generous heart earned him the position of the 11th President of India! Despite holding the highest position in office, Kalam chose to live a simple life, never forgetting his humble origin.

To promote equality, he mingled and mixed with everyone. He included common people in presidential programs, and made efforts to hear the voice of those who were ignored. For this, Kalam was known as the People's President.

Kalam had a strong artistic side - he authored many books, wrote a lot of poetry in Tamil and was very fond of playing the veena. Among his most treasured possessions was a collection of over 2,500 books.

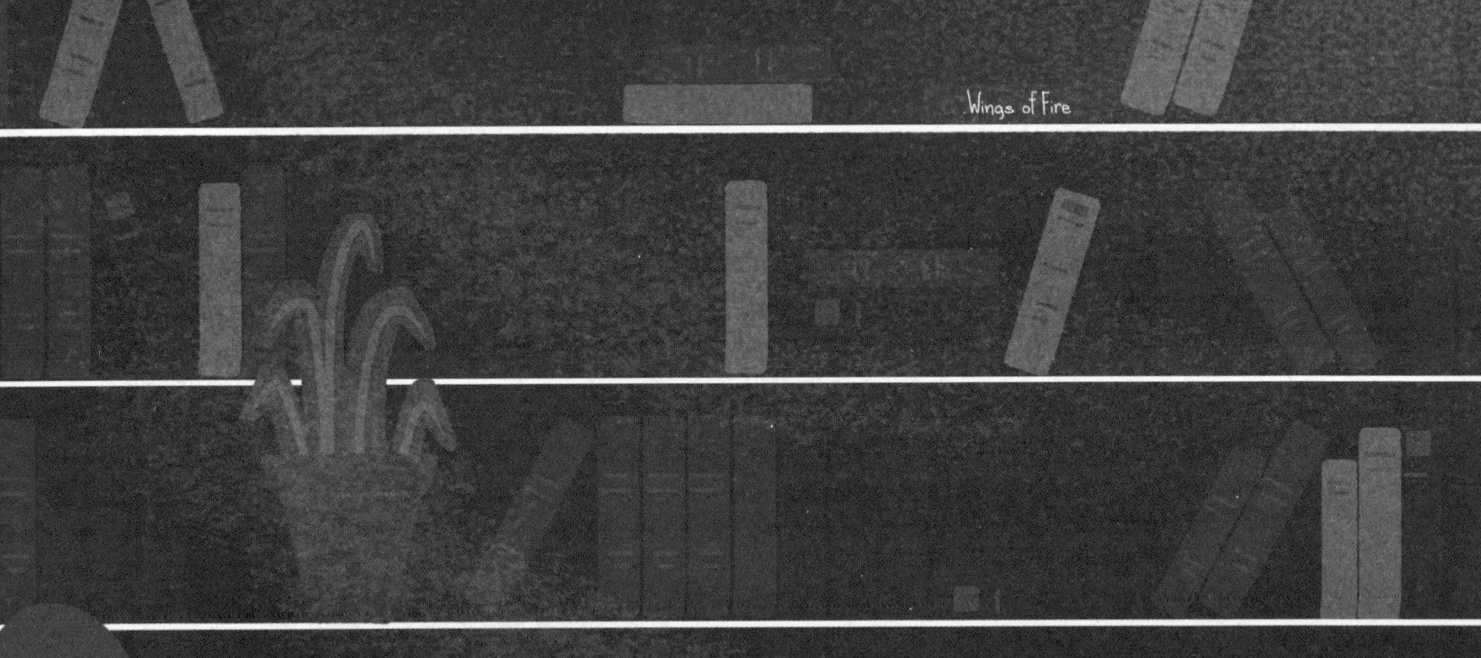

Tamil Poetry

Poetry

Abdul Kalam authored many books, including - India 2020, Ignited Minds, Mission India, Inspiring Thoughts and an autobiography titled Wings of Fire.

Always wanting to be remembered as a teacher, he loved interacting with students while giving lectures at many reputed colleges across the world.

On July 27th, 2015, Abdul Kalam died from a heart attack at the age of 83, while doing what he loved most - speaking to students at the Indian Institute of Management in Shillong.

From Abdul Kalam's magnificent life, we can learn that anyone can do great things, irrespective of the obstacles in front of them, if they work hard enough and dream big enough. Kalam will always be remembered as a simple and compassionate man who devoted his immense knowledge to serving India.

LEARN MORE

Before Abdul Kalam took the initiative of supervising Pokhran-II, India's earlier nuclear test happened way back in 1974. An Indian Ministry of Defence program, the Integrated Guided Missile Development Programme was also started under Abdul Kalam's leadership, and ended in 2008 after the successful development of several important missiles, including the following:

- PRITHVI - short range surface-to-surface ballistic missile

- TRISHUL - short range low-level surface-to-air missile

- AKASH - medium range surface-to-air missile

- NAG - third-generation anti-tank missile

- AGNI - intermediate range surface-to-surface ballistic missile

Have you heard these famous quotes by Abdul Kalam?

JOIN THE DOTS

Starting from 1, join the dots to reveal an image of Prithvi!

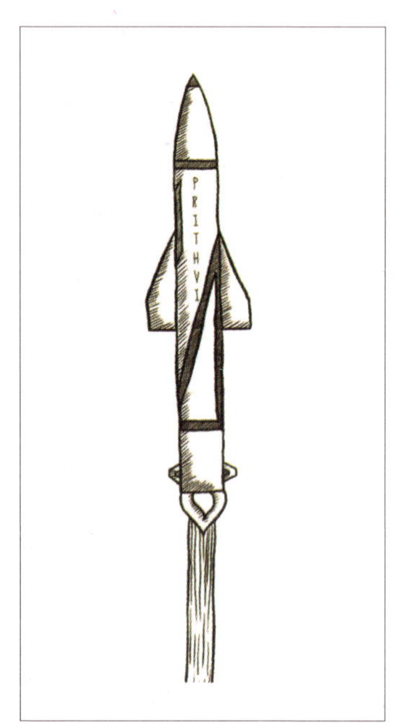

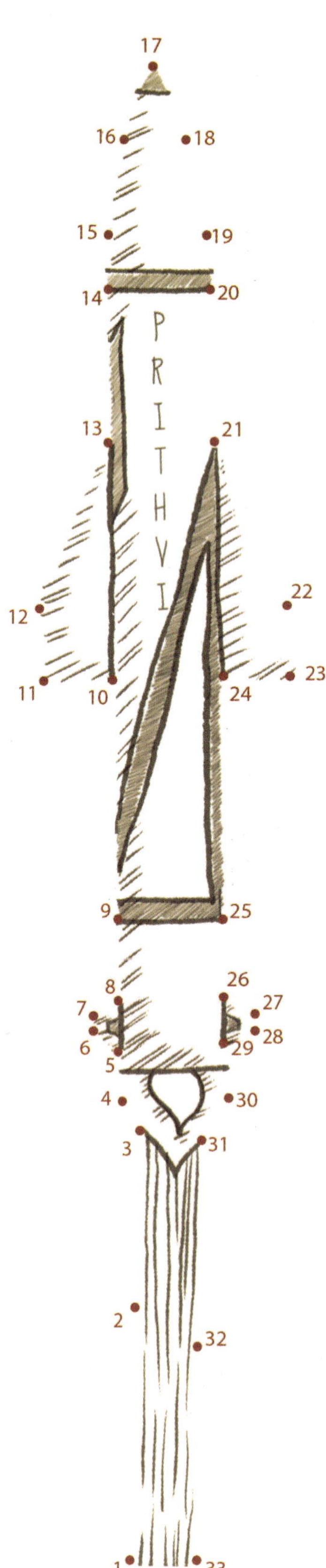